Food Webs

Rainforest Food Chains

Emma Lynch

Heinemann Library
Chicago, Illinois

© 2005 Heinemann Library
a division of Reed Elsevier Inc.
Chicago, Illinois

Customer Service   888–454–2279

Visit our website at www.heinemannlibrary.com

Photo research by Ruth Blair and Ginny Stroud-Lewis
Designed by Jo Hinton-Malivoire and AMR
Printed in China by WKT Company Limited.

09 08 07 06 05
10 9 8 7 6 5 4 3 2 1

Library of Congress Cataloging-in-Publication Data
Lynch, Emma.
  Rainforest food chains / Emma Lynch.
     v. cm. — (Food webs)
  Includes bibliographical references and index.
  Contents: What is a rainforest food web? — What is a rainforest food chain? — What is a producer in a rainforest? — What is a primary consumer in a rainforest? — What is a secondary consumer in a rainforest? — What is a decomposer in a rainforest? — How are rainforest food chains different in different places? — What Happens to a food web when a food chain breaks down? — How can we protect the environment and rainforest food chains?
  ISBN 1-4034-5858-8 (lib. bdg.) — ISBN 1-4034-5865-0 (pbk.)
  1. Rain forest ecology—Juvenile literature. 2. Food chains (Ecology)—Juvenile literature. [1. Rain forest ecology. 2. Food chains (Ecology) 3. Ecology.] I. Title. II. Series.
  QH541.5.R27L96 2004
  577.34—dc22

                              2003026199

Acknowledgments
The author and publisher are grateful to the following for permission to reproduce copyright material:
a-z botanicals p. **12**; Corbis pp. **5** (Bob Krist), **8** (Tom Brakefield), **11** (Matt Brown), **13** (Kevin Schafer), **14** (Jack Fields), **15** (Kennan Ward), **17** (Martin Rogers), **19** (Arne Hodalic), **25** (Natalie Fobes), **26** (Alison Wright), **27** (M. Sinibaldi); Heather Angel/Natural Visions pp. **7, 18** (Brian Rogers); Nature Picture Library pp. **10** (Peter Oxford), **16** (Doug Allan); NHPA p. **23**.

Cover photograph of a toucan eating fruit reproduced with permission of Bruce Coleman/ Staffan Widstrand.

Illustrations by Words and Publications.

The publisher would like to thank Dr Dennis Radabaugh of the Department of Zoology at Ohio Wesleyan University for his comments in the preparation of this book.

Contents

Some words are shown in bold, **like this**. You can find out
what they mean by looking in the glossary.

What Is a Rainforest Food Web?

All living things, including plants, **fungi**, humans, and other animals, are **organisms**. Each organism is eaten by another organism. Small animals are eaten by bigger animals, and then these animals get eaten by even larger ones. When large animals die, they get eaten by tiny insects, maggots, and **bacteria**. Even mighty trees die and rot, and are eaten by beetles, grubs, and fungi. If you draw lines between the organisms, showing who eats who, you create a diagram called a food web. It looks like a tangled spider's web!

In rainforests, just as in all **habitats**, the organisms that live there are connected as parts of a food web. In food web diagrams, the arrow leads from the food to the animal that eats it.

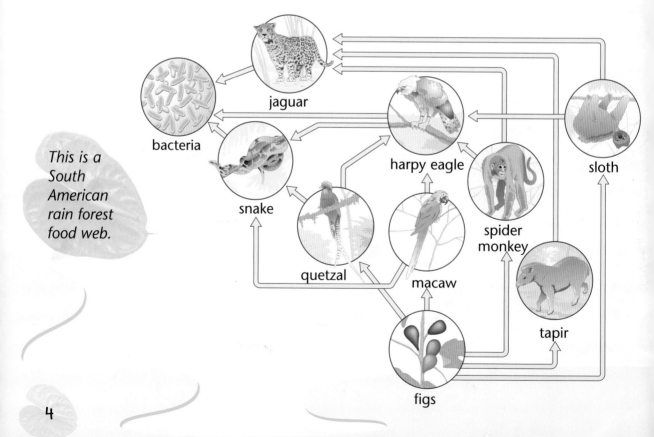

This is a South American rain forest food web.

jaguar

bacteria

snake

harpy eagle

sloth

spider monkey

quetzal

macaw

tapir

figs

4

What are rainforest habitats like?

This book looks at the food web and food chains of rain forest habitats. Rain forests are found in places with a **tropical climate**, usually near the **equator**. The climate is hot, and there is heavy rainfall all through the year.

Certain plants and animals live in the rain forest because they are especially suited to life there, and because the plants or animals that they feed on live there. Some, like mosses and jaguars, live on the forest floor. Plants such as vines and palms live in the dark **understory**. Animals such as monkeys and sloths live in the trees. Birds such as the harpy eagle fly through the treetops, called the **canopy** level, or above the forest, looking for animals to catch and eat.

This rainforest habitat is in the Caribbean island of Grenada.

What Is a Rainforest Food Chain?

A food web looks quite complex, but it is actually made up of many simpler food chains. These food chains show the way some of the organisms in a food web feed on each other. The arrows in the chain show the movement of food and **energy** from plants to animals as they feed on each other. More than half of the world's animal and plant **species** live in **tropical** rainforests, so the rainforest food web is made up of millions of food chains.

An **organism** can be part of more than one food chain in a food web. Most animals eat more than one type of food, because they have a better chance of survival if they do not depend on just one food source. They will also probably be eaten by more than one kind of animal!

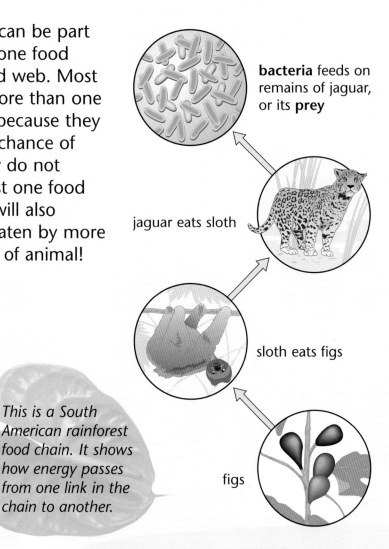

bacteria feeds on remains of jaguar, or its **prey**

jaguar eats sloth

sloth eats figs

figs

This is a South American rainforest food chain. It shows how energy passes from one link in the chain to another.

Starting the chain

Most food chains start with the energy that comes from the Sun. Plants take in water from the soil through their roots and **carbon dioxide** from the air through their leaves. Their leaves also trap the energy from sunlight and use this to change the water and carbon dioxide into sugary food. This process is called **photosynthesis**. Plants use this food, along with **nutrients** from the soil, to grow.

Every part of a growing plant can become food for other organisms in the **habitat**. They can eat the plant's roots, shoots, leaves, nuts, fruit, bark—or even the rotten plant when it has died. Animals cannot make their own food, so they eat the plants to get energy. Plant-eating animals may be eaten by other bigger animals that get energy from them. In this way, the energy flows through the food chain and through the habitat.

*Rainforest trees spread a dense **canopy** of leaves to catch as much of the Sun's light as they can.*

Making the chain

Plants are called **producers**, because they trap the Sun's **energy** and make, or produce, food for themselves and other animals. Producers provide food for plant-eating animals, known as **herbivores**. In food chains, herbivores are **primary consumers**. Primary consumers are often food for other animals we call **carnivores**. In food chains, these carnivores are **secondary consumers**. Secondary consumers catch and eat primary consumers, and they may also eat other smaller secondary consumers.

Animals that eat both plants and other animals are called **omnivores**. Omnivores can be primary and secondary consumers.

Squirrel monkeys are omnivores. They eat mainly flowers, fruits, and seeds, but also insects and other small animals.

More links in the chain

Food chains usually start with producers, and then go on to primary consumers and secondary consumers. But the chain does not end there. All **organisms** eventually die. When that happens, animals called **scavengers**, including worms and maggots, eat their bodies. **Decomposers** such as **bacteria** and **fungi** then eat or break down any dead remains that are left. They also eat or break down rotting trees and plants. The waste from these decomposers sinks into the soil or riverbed, where some of it becomes **nutrients** that can be taken in by plant roots. In this way, the chain begins again.

This food chain from the Amazon rainforest shows how energy moves from producer to consumer to decomposer.

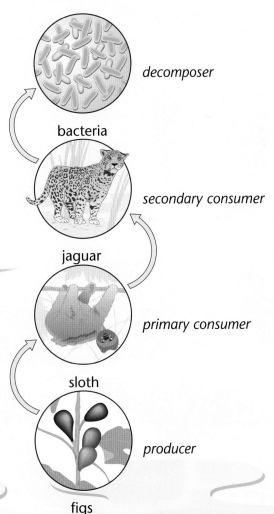

decomposer

bacteria

secondary consumer

jaguar

primary consumer

sloth

producer

figs

Breaking the chain

If some of the **organisms** in a food web die out, it may be deadly for other organisms in the web. Sometimes natural events can damage a food web, but more often in the case of rainforests, human activity is the biggest danger. Rainforests are cut down either for their wood or to make space for cattle or businesses. This is deadly for the animals of the rainforest, because they lose their food supplies, **habitat**, and shelter. **Pollution** from businesses can also break rainforest food chains and other natural cycles, with terrible results.

Forest fires can sometimes be started by lightning strikes. Such natural events can harm food webs by destroying large areas of rainforest.

Which Producers Live in Rainforests?

Plants are **producers**, and they are at the start of most rainforest food chains. There are many producers in a rainforest **habitat**. Some plants grow on the forest floor, such as shrubs and moss. Ferns, vines, palms, and creepers can grow in the **understory**, since they do not need much light to survive. They provide food and shelter for insects, birds, and small **rodents**. Up in the trees, the leaves, bark, fruit, and nuts provide food for monkeys, birds, and insects. Other plants called **epiphytes** grow on the trees. They get their **nutrients** from air, rainwater, and waste material on the branches where they grow.

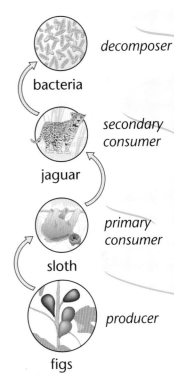

decomposer

bacteria

secondary consumer

jaguar

primary consumer

sloth

producer

figs

Mosses and ferns cover the floor of the rainforest and the lower parts of the trees.

Many rainforest **producers** also have brightly colored flowers and fruit that grow high up at the **canopy** level. These are important foods for the parrots and butterflies that live in this part of the rainforest. The insects and birds **pollinate** the flowers.

These fruits of the black bean plant are eaten by the insects and birds that live in the canopy of the Australian rainforest.

Breaking the Chain: Producers

Green plants are extremely important to rainforest food chains, but they are in grave danger. It is thought that over 200,000 acres (80,000 hectares) of rainforest are burned down every day around the world—that's 150 acres (60 hectares) of trees, with all the plant life that grows on and around them, lost every minute. Without those trees and plants, there is no food and shelter for the animals that depend on them. Even the soil the trees grow in soon becomes poor. Thousands of **species** are at risk of **extinction**.

Which Primary Consumers Live in Rainforests?

Primary consumers in the rainforest can be small or large animals that live on the forest floor and up in the trees. They feed on the rich plant life of the forest, from the fruit, flowers, and leaves of the trees, to the shrubs and moss that grow at ground level.

On the Amazon forest floor, insects such as leaf-cutting ants and beetles search for food, nibbling the leaves and **fungi**. Ground **rodents** such as agoutis and pacas travel through the forest at night, hunting for plants to eat.

Larger primary consumers include the tapir, a piglike animal with a long, bendy nose. Tapirs spend their days among the low-growing plants, but come out at night to feed on leaves and fruit. They often cover themselves in a layer of mud, as a protection from insect bites!

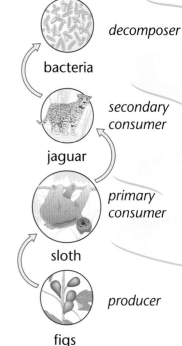

decomposer

bacteria

secondary consumer

jaguar

primary consumer

sloth

producer

figs

*This Baird's tapir is munching on Amazon rainforest plants. There are four species of tapirs, and all of them are now **endangered**.*

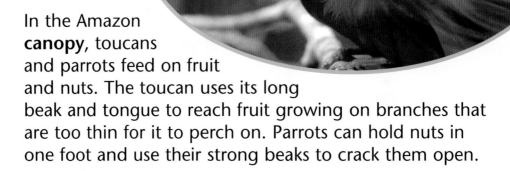

*This male great bird of paradise is from Papua New Guinea, in southeastern Asia. There are over 40 **species** of these birds. Most eat a mixture of insects and fruit.*

In the Amazon **canopy**, toucans and parrots feed on fruit and nuts. The toucan uses its long beak and tongue to reach fruit growing on branches that are too thin for it to perch on. Parrots can hold nuts in one foot and use their strong beaks to crack them open.

Fruit bats sleep all day, then come out at night to feed on fruit, **nectar**, and **pollen**. Brightly colored butterflies flutter through the trees, feeding on the nectar in their flowers. Hummingbirds are also nectar feeders. Their wings move so fast that they are a blur. They hover in midair as they dip their long bills into flowers.

The three-toed sloth is a strange and slow-moving animal that hangs from the branches of trees—even when it is asleep—and grinds leaves very slowly in its teeth. Its hairy coat is green from the mosses and tiny plants that grow on it. It blends in with the leaves, and moves so slowly that **predators** have a hard time spotting it. If a jaguar sees a sloth, it will try to climb up and catch it.

Which Secondary Consumers Live in Rainforests?

Secondary consumers can be **carnivores** or **omnivores**. A carnivore's food is rich in **nutrients** but is not always easy to catch, so predators must put a lot of **energy** into hunting their **prey**. Big cats like the jaguar, ocelot, and margay are rainforest predators.

Jaguars are the largest secondary consumers in the Amazon rainforest. They prowl around the forest floor and will eat any animal they find. Jaguars like to eat tapirs, but they also eat monkeys, water birds, caimans, and tortoises.

The largest flying predator in the Amazon rainforest is the huge harpy eagle. Harpy eagles soar over the treetops, then swoop down to snatch prey with their strong claws, called talons. They also eat other birds, monkeys, and sloths.

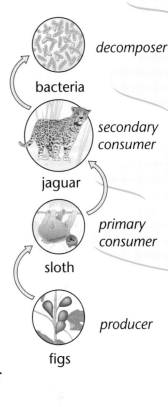

decomposer

bacteria

secondary consumer

jaguar

primary consumer

sloth

producer

figs

Jaguars are good swimmers and will even follow their prey into water.

The giant anaconda is one of the largest snakes in the world. It lives along the banks of the Amazon River and eats **mammals** and birds that go there to drink. It drags them under the water, where it kills and swallows them. Anacondas can climb as well as swim, and hide from their **prey** in the rainforest trees.

The deep flower of this Madagascar pitcher plant is a deadly trap for careless insects.

Sometimes plants can be **predators**, too! There are some rainforest plants, such as the pitcher plant, that trap small insects and spiders. They invite the insects into their cup-shaped leaves by leaving **nectar** at the top of the "cup." The insects fall into the plant but cannot get back out. The plant takes in the **nutrients** from the insects' bodies to help it grow.

Omnivores hunt for prey, but they also eat many kinds of plants. In the Australian rainforest, the bandicoot feeds on fruits, or may dig its snout and claws into the ground to find insects to eat. It also eats small mammals.

Which Decomposers Live in Rainforests?

Every acre of rainforest is filled with about two tons (about 2 tonnes) of plant and animal waste every year. If this dead matter and waste just stayed on the ground, air and water could not get through to the tree roots, and nutrients would not be recycled for plants to use as food. However, the **decomposers** and **scavengers** on the forest floor help to recycle all the waste matter. When plants and animals die, decomposers break down the decaying matter into simpler substances, such as **carbon dioxide** and water.

In the rainforest, this recycling happens faster than anywhere else on Earth, because of the high temperature and the large amount of moisture in the air. The main rainforest decomposers are **fungi** and tiny **organisms** such as **bacteria**.

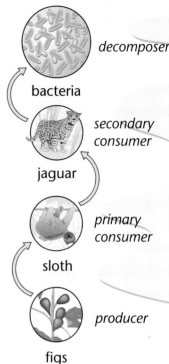

decomposer

bacteria

secondary consumer

jaguar

primary consumer

sloth

producer

figs

These bracket fungi are growing on a tree stump in Costa Rica. The "brackets" are only a small part of the fungus. A network of tiny tubes spreads deep inside the wood.

When a tree falls to the rainforest floor, it is quickly covered with insects and **fungi** that eat the wood and bark. Termites are especially helpful **scavengers** in the rainforest because they are very good wood eaters. The holes and tunnels that termites dig provide a way for **decomposers** such as fungi to get deep into the wood. These insects and decomposers work so well that a dead branch in the rainforest disappears completely in just a week or two.

When an animal dies in the rainforest, fungi and **bacteria** soon decompose it, with the help of earthworms. The animal's body rots and lets out **nutrients**. These sink into the soil of the rainforest floor and are taken in by the plants, making them able to start their life processes all over again.

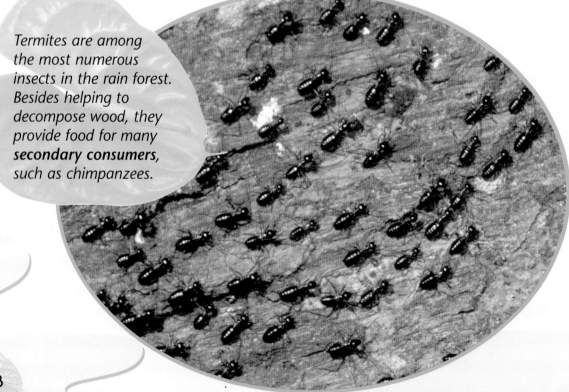

*Termites are among the most numerous insects in the rain forest. Besides helping to decompose wood, they provide food for many **secondary consumers**, such as chimpanzees.*

How Are Rainforest Food Chains Different in Different Places?

There are rainforests all over the world—in South America, southeastern Asia, Australia, and central Africa. Although these rainforests share similar **climates** and thick forests, the food chains can be very different. Food chains depend on the location of the rainforest and the plants and animals that live there. Human activity also affects the food chains.

The Australian rainforest is small, but it is home to some remarkable animals, including this cassowary bird.

The Amazon rainforest

The Amazon rainforest is the largest in the world. It runs through Central and South America and covers approximately 1.6 million square miles (4.1 million square kilometers) in Brazil alone. More than 4,000 **species** of trees live here, some more than 164 feet (50 meters) high. Over 500 species of birds search for fruit and nuts to eat. There are brightly colored toucans, macaws, and parrots, and tiny hummingbirds searching for flowers. Many species of monkeys also live here, from the tiny squirrel monkey to the large howler monkey. Boa constrictors and emerald boas slide along tree branches, watching out for frogs and lizards to eat.

On the forest floor, **predators** hunt in the shadows while huge groups of army ants march across the ground looking for food. Every year, the Amazon River floods across much of the forest, forming the largest river basin in the world. Thousands of freshwater fish swim here, including sharp-toothed piranhas.

The African rainforest

The belt of rainforest that stretches across central Africa is the second largest rainforest in the world. It is home to an amazing variety of animals. Elephants, gorillas, and chimpanzees live at or near ground level. Leopards hunt here, too. Up in the trees, colobus monkeys leap from branch to branch, while hornbills and parrots search for insects and fruit. The crowned eagle hunts up in the **canopy**.

The colobus monkey eats 4.5–6 pounds (2–3 kilograms) of leaves every day. This is about one-quarter of its body weight. To keep this up, the animal has to spend about a third of its day eating.

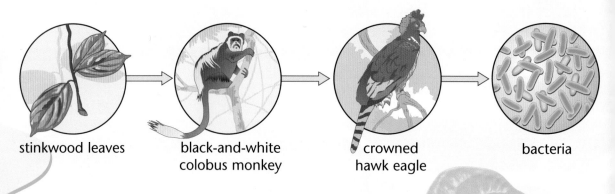

stinkwood leaves   black-and-white   crowned   bacteria
                      colobus monkey   hawk eagle

The African rain forest includes this food chain.

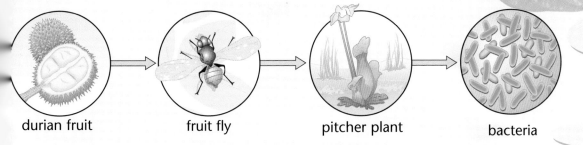

durian fruit   fruit fly   pitcher plant   bacteria

The southeastern Asian rainforest

The rainforests of southeastern Asia occur in patches, not in one large area like the Amazon rain forest. They are found in countries like Malaysia and on islands such as Borneo and Sumatra. Borneo is one of the few places in the region where there are still large sections of rain forest that have not been spoiled by farming, wars, or cutting down trees.

These forests have a huge variety of plants and animals. Rain forest trees reach up toward the sunlight, surrounded by vines such as lianas and covered by other **epiphytes**. Many of the insects are big and brightly colored. The stink bug and the atlas moth live among the leaves of the trees. Ants live inside the Malaysian epiphyte *Myrmecodia*. In return for their shelter, the ants protect the plant from plant-eating insects. Durian trees here produce some of the smelliest fruits in the world, and brightly colored **fungi** grow throughout the forests.

Pitcher plants are among the **carnivores** in the southeastern Asian rain forest. Their cup-shaped leaves with **nectar** along their rims invite insects, who then fall into the cup. There they are broken down by the plant.

What Happens to a Food Web When a Food Chain Breaks Down?

All around the world, rainforest food chains and webs are in danger because of humans. Although much work is being done to stop further harm, plants and animals in rainforest **habitats** face many problems today.

Habitat destruction

Rainforests once covered 14 percent of Earth's surface, but they now cover only 6 percent. In less than 50 years, more than half of the world's rainforests have been destroyed, and this pace keeps increasing. Over 200,000 acres (80,000 hectares) of rainforest are lost every day, as trees are cut down to use for fuel or wood, and to provide land where cattle can graze. Cutting down trees, called logging, is destroying the habitat for wildlife. There are fewer animals because there are fewer plants to hide them from **predators** and hunters. Animals are being driven farther into the rainforest to find new homes.

Scientists think that at this rate the last remaining rainforests could be destroyed in less than 40 years. Scientists also believe that about 130 **species** of plants, animals, and insects are becoming **extinct** every single day, often before scientists have even studied them.

Pollution

The Amazon rainforest is also at risk of **pollution** from people digging for metals, an activity called mining. Brazil is rich in metals, and there are many groups doing mining there. However, some of the chemicals used in mining, such as gold, nickel, and copper, run into rivers and streams in the region and are carried hundreds of miles. This pollution poisons plants and animals on and near the river, or drives them away from their natural **habitat**.

Overhunting

Many rainforest animals are at risk from overfishing and overhunting. In the central African rainforest, the western lowland gorilla and the chimpanzee are **endangered** animals. Both have been hunted, and their habitat continues to be destroyed. If they are not protected, they will be gone forever.

In the central African rainforest, the male silverback gorilla is the leading member of his group.

Global warming

Rainforests have been called the lungs of the planet. The trees in the rainforest help us to breathe by giving off the gas oxygen into the air. They also take in large amounts of **carbon dioxide**, a gas that is not good for us to breathe, from the air during **photosynthesis**. This helps to remove some of the carbon dioxide that humans produce by burning oil and coal. When forests are cut down, there are fewer trees to take in carbon dioxide. This could make Earth hotter and cause great harm to all living things.

Breaking the Chain: How We Are Affected

When animals and plants are poisoned, killed, or driven out of their natural **habitat**, it breaks the food chains and affects the entire food web of the region. In the end, breaks or changes to food chains and webs affect humans, too. We can have problems caused by **pollution** and mercury poisoning. When rainforests are cut down, there are fewer plants to keep the air clean, and Earth gets slowly warmer. Humans along the Amazon River have fewer fish to catch and eat. Protecting and caring for rainforest food webs is important for all living things.

How Can We Protect Rainforest Food Chains?

All around the world, scientists, governments, and other groups are working to protect rainforests and rainforest food chains. They want to be sure that no more harm is done to these habitats and the animals and plants that depend on them to survive.

International research and protection

Scientists and **conservation** workers make surveys of rainforest habitats. They keep track of animal and plant life in the rainforests to check that their numbers do not fall. In this way, scientists find the links in the food web that need protection.

Conservation workers will study this Komodo dragon at their research center.

Scientists suggest ways that governments can improve and protect rainforest **habitats** while still making the money they need out of them. Groups like Friends of the Earth, Greenpeace, and the World Wildlife Fund work to make governments take care of rainforests and to make sure people know when problems arise. They try to stop illegal logging and suggest other ways to manage forests.

In the Amazon, scientists, plant collectors, **conservation** workers, and companies that make medicines are studying plants. They want to prove that some rainforest plants can be used for making important drugs and cures. These uses could make more money for countries than they could earn by chopping down the rainforests.

Conservation groups also run projects to teach people living in or near rainforests about how they can help to protect them, now and in the future.

Many groups are working hard to help conserve the world's rainforests. Fifteen percent of the Amazon rainforest is at risk from logging like this.

Research a forest food web in your local area

You can study forest habitats in your local area, even though they are not exactly the same as a rainforest. If you go on a trip to a forest, think about the food chains of that habitat. Here are some suggestions to help you find out about animal and plant life and some tips to help you protect the habitat where they live.

1. What is the habitat like? Is it cold, warm, shady, or light? How is it different from a rainforest?
2. What plants and animals live there? Try to put them in groups that are similar, such as plants, insects, birds, and **mammals**.
3. What do you think each animal would like to eat?
4. Which are the **predators** and which are the **prey**?
5. Can you make a food chain of the animals and plants you see?
6. Think about how the habitat could change. How would these changes affect the wildlife there?

Thousands of plants, animals, and insects live in forest habitats, living on or near the forest trees.

27

Where Are the World's Main Rainforests?

This map shows the location of the major rainforests of the world.

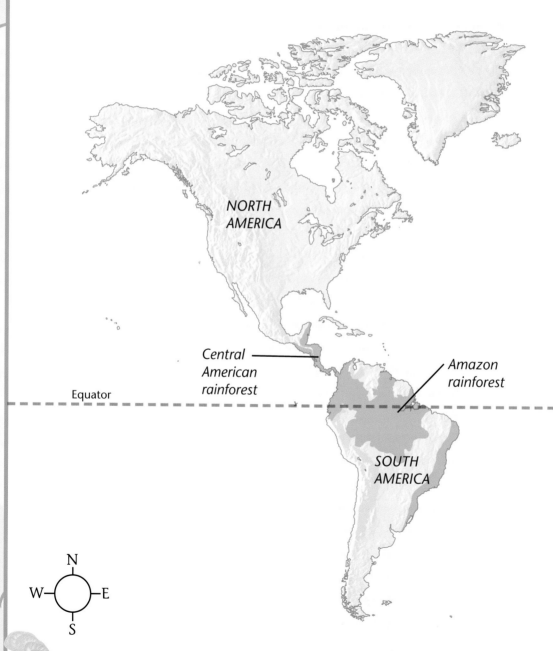

NORTH AMERICA

Central American rainforest

Amazon rainforest

Equator

SOUTH AMERICA

N
W — E
S

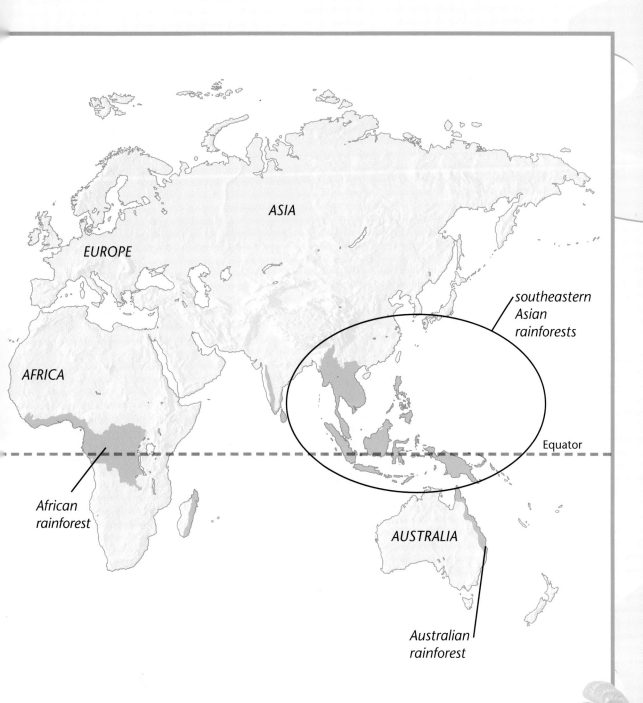

ASIA

EUROPE

AFRICA

southeastern
Asian
rainforests

Equator

African
rainforest

AUSTRALIA

Australian
rainforest

29

Glossary

bacteria (singular bacterium) tiny living decomposers found everywhere

canopy layer of trees near the top of the rainforest

carbon dioxide gas in the air that animals breathe out and plants use to make food

carnivore animal that eats the flesh of another animal

climate general conditions of weather in an area

conservation protecting and saving the natural environment

decomposer organism that breaks down and gets nutrients from dead plants and animals and their waste

endangered at risk of dying out completely, as a species of animal or plant

energy power to grow, move, and do things

epiphyte plant that grows above the ground, using other plants or objects for support but not harming them

equator imaginary line around the Earth, equally distant from the north and south poles

extinct died out completely

fungi (singular fungus) group of decomposer organisms including mushrooms, toadstools, and their relatives

habitat place where an organism lives

herbivore animal that eats plants

mammal animal that feeds its babies on milk from its own body

nectar sugary substance made by plants to attract insects that eat it

nutrient chemical that plants and animals need to live

omnivore animal that eats both plants and other animals

organism living thing

photosynthesis process by which plants make their own food using carbon dioxide, water, and energy from sunlight

pollen small grains that are the male parts of a flower. Pollen combines with eggs (female flower parts) to form seeds.

pollinate to carry pollen from the male part of a flower to a female part

pollution when chemicals or other substances that can damage animal or plant life escape into water, soil, or the air

predator animal that hunts and eats other animals

prey animal that is caught and eaten by a predator

primary consumer animal that eats plants

producer organism (plant) that can make its own food

rodent mammal with large gnawing front teeth, such as a mouse or rat

scavenger organism that feeds on dead plant and animal material and waste

secondary consumer animal that eats primary consumers and other secondary consumers

species group of organisms that are similar to each other and can breed together to produce young

tropical belonging to a region of the world that is warm all year round but has one or more rainy seasons

understory dark part of the rainforest, above the forest floor but below the canopy, where only plants that do not need much light can grow

More Books to Read

Baker, Lucy. *Life in the Rain Forests.* Santa Monica, CA: Creative Publishing, 2003.

Baldwin, Carol. *Living in a Rain Forest.* Chicago, IL: Heinemann Library, 2003.

Greenaway, Theresa. *Food Chains.* Chicago, IL: Raintree, 2001.

Johansson, Philip. *The Tropical Rain Forest.* Berkeley Heights, NJ: Enslow Publishers, 2004.

Lauber, Patricia. *Who Eats What?* New York: HarperCollins, 2001.

Llewellyn, Claire. *Animal Atlas.* Santa Monica, CA: Creative Publishing, 2003.

Morey, Allan. *Rain Forest Food Chains.* Minneapolis, MN: Lake Street Publishers, 2003.

Morgan, Sally. *Saving the Rainforests.* Danbury, CT: Scholastic Library, 1999.

Pirotta, Saviour. *Predators in the Rain Forest.* Chicago, IL: Raintree, 1999.

Pirotta, Saviour. *Trees and Plants in the Rain Forest.* Chicago, IL: Raintree, 1999.

Index